CREATE YOUR IDEAL FUTURE

*Simple Tools to Form
Powerful Habits*

ASHLEY SHAW

Copyright © 2025 Ashley Shaw
All Rights Reserved.

Acknowledgments

To my husband, Terald, your love, prayers, and encouragement have been my steadfast foundation. Your unwavering support and belief in me have been a source of unending strength. Thank you for being my partner in every sense of the word.

To my beloved sons, Harrison and Bryson, you are the light of my life. Your curiosity and boundless energy inspire me daily to be the best version of myself.

To my parents, Rick McPherson and Dema Newby, for instilling in me the values of determination and resilience; to my sister, Candace Hildebran, for your boundless encouragement and belief in me; and to my extended family: my nanny, aunts, uncles, and cousins, thank you for your love and the innumerable ways you've supported me throughout my journey. To my niece, Alonna, and nephews: Collin, Evan, Parker, and Jonah—I love you so very much.

To my incredible friends and colleagues, your encouragement and understanding have been invaluable. Your cheerleading has lifted me during the hard times and celebrated with me during the highs. Thank you for believ-ing in me and this project and thank you for your friendship. Thank you to Danielle Culbreath, Maria VonDielingen, Cassandra Martin, Nolan King, Haley Hill, Heather Powell, Tanise Love, Melissa Jackson, Maria Ortiz, Brett Rettenmund, and so many more.

Each of you has been a part of this journey, and I am profoundly grateful for your encouragement and contributions that made this book possible.

Most of all, I want to thank God, because without Him, I wouldn't be able to do any of this. Initially, I hesitated to write this book. It wasn't a personal ambition or a task I readily embraced. Instead, it was a calling that I felt deeply from God.

Despite my initial reluctance and the begrudging manner in which I began, a transformation occurred. Gradually, the purpose behind this endeavor unfolded before my eyes.

I came to understand that there are countless individuals who can benefit from the message this book holds—people who are struggling while not realizing how much power they possess. Through this journey of obedience and faith, my hopes and prayers are that this book reaches those people. That it serves its intended purpose and has a profound impact in the lives of those it touches.

Contents

CHAPTER 1
Taking Ownership — 3

CHAPTER 2
The Power of Choice — 12

CHAPTER 3
Progress over Perfection — 21

CHAPTER 4
Choose Your Habits Wisely — 29

CHAPTER 5
Consistency is Key — 37

CHAPTER 6
Mindset Matters — 45

CHAPTER 7
Watch Your Words — 53

CHAPTER 8
Believing in Yourself — 61

CHAPTER 9
Show Me Your Friends, I'll Show You Your Future — 72

CHAPTER 10
Conclusion — Make It Count — 81

Welcome, dear reader!

Regardless of where you find yourself today, my hope is that the message in this book abundantly blesses you. Whether you're currently at rock bottom and looking for a glimmer of hope, or you're just in a spot where you feel you're not progressing through life as much as you'd like, this book is for you!

I was once in a place where I was stumbling through life, making poor choices, and wondering how I ended up in such a mess. I had a wake-up call, a moment that changed everything (more on that later). I am grateful for this wake-up call as it pushed me onto a new path, one filled with better decisions that redirected my entire life. Thankfully, I had this wake-up call early on; regardless of what stage of life you are in, it is never too late.

I can proudly say that I love the life I live today. I am happily married, have two beautiful sons, meaningful friendships, and I've built a successful career. More importantly, I've had the chance to help numerous people gain clarity on what they truly want and establish the habits needed to reach their goals. This journey has filled me with gratitude, and I've been encouraged by many to share my story and insights through this book.

I believe I've been called by God to spread a message of hope and empowerment. My aim is to encourage you to form powerful habits so you can live a life that's truly your own—a life you are proud of.

Join me as we explore how even the smallest choices can create big changes. Together, we'll work toward unlocking the life you dream of living.

With warmth and determination,
Ashley Shaw

CHAPTER 1
Taking Ownership

The Night That Changed My Life

The summer before my senior year of high school was meant to be all about fun and freedom. Instead, it became a major turning point in my life. Hanging out with friends, hopping from one party to the next was the norm. With my trusty mix of vodka and Sprite—vodka I swiped from the local CVS, you know, being seventeen and all—I felt invincible. Driving wasn't off the table either, despite the countless nights I did so under the influence, foolishly convinced nothing would happen to me.

In a small town, everyone knows everyone else's business, and our antics weren't hard to spot. I was definitely mixed up in all the wrong things. I was missing school, drinking alcohol, and basically doing everything I shouldn't and nothing that I should. My wake-up call came one night with the blare of police sirens filling the air, their colors bright in my rearview mirror, and the inconvenient truth of my actions crashing down on me. The officer didn't bother with formalities: as soon as he saw me, he asked,

"Are you Ashley McPherson?" Talk about a reality check. That was the moment I realized how well-known I'd become for all the wrong reasons.

Blowing a 0.75 on the breathalyzer meant real trouble—not just because it was illegal due to my age but because it signified a step too far down the wrong path. That night became a pivotal moment for me. I remember lying in the bed of my jail cell the first night and thanking God for saving me. I realized that I was on a destructive path that would ultimately lead to either a life of addiction or ultimately, death. Inside a juvenile detention center for three weeks, with nothing but time to think, it became a turning point in my life. That's when it hit me: maybe getting arrested wasn't a disaster, but a chance to turn things around. I started feeling grateful for this wake-up call, for a shot at starting fresh.

The return home marked a huge shift in my relationships, especially my family's trust. It hit so hard that my mom set me up with a babysitter that summer. I was seventeen years old and being dropped off at my aunt's house each day as my mom went to work, since I could not be trusted to be alone. As embarrassing as it was, it was necessary. Although I will say my Aunt Donna is super cool and we really enjoyed each other's company that summer.

Throughout the summer and into the school year, Probation made sure I could not forget the mess I had made, with its constant demands and random drug tests. Instead of letting it pull me down, I used these reminders to fuel my determination to change.

When it was time to head back to school, I was armed with a new attitude. My decision to try my best came from understanding that I did not want to be stuck in the same old patterns. The problem was, I didn't know what steps I was going to take to make my life better. I didn't have any particular process to follow or tools to implement. I just knew that I was going to say no to drugs and alcohol, show up to school and do the work—no more turning in blank assignments and tests. Around that time, I started going to church and reading my Bible. That is when my life really started to change and I could see God opening doors for me.

Early on in my senior year of high school, someone had told me that they heard it was possible to get off of probation early if you got accepted into college. One minor problem, I had a 1.9 GPA and had missed so much school that I had to make up significant hours in order to be able to even graduate. Thankfully, I learned about the Groups Program at Indiana University. The Groups Program is for first generation college students. They give students that might not otherwise have access to higher education the opportunity to earn a seat at the best school in God's country, Indiana University. They require you to attend a six-week college prep "camp" on campus the summer before your freshman year; they pay for your first year, then give you an opportunity to earn scholarships based on your GPA.

As soon as I found out about this program, I applied. Going to college was more than just school for me; it was a way to start fresh in life. Growing up, I didn't have the expectation of going to college since neither of my parents finished high school. They wanted my sister and me to do better than they did, so they always encouraged us to graduate from high school. My parents have always been hardworking, loving, and supportive, but higher education was never talked about in our family. When I told them I was going to college, they were certainly surprised, but also really proud.

I am extremely grateful for the Groups Program because it became my gateway to a new beginning. It offered a chance not only to be the first in my family to get a college education, but to redefine who I wanted to be. Participating in their six-week prep course was about more than academics; it was about life. I plunged into it headfirst, determined to shift my path from reckless choices to achievements I could be proud of.

Maybe my story hits home for you in some way. You might have recently hit rock bottom or you could just be fed up with mediocrity. Either way, this chapter is an invitation to move from merely thinking about change to truly committing to it. Throughout my journey of moving from a detention cell to a college campus, I discovered a powerful truth: every choice I make builds my future. Owning my mistakes and being aware of my actions gave me control over my life. And I want the same for you. Please know that ownership is step one. It's easy to point fingers and blame, but real freedom and growth come from owning up to your decisions.

We can all have a tendency to deflect ownership and find someone to blame, especially when there is bad news. Think about it, when a family member has a health event, it is not uncommon that we try to point blame at doctors and how they could have handled things differently. Or if a child gets in trouble, their natural response is to blame their sibling or some other external factor. It starts at a young age. We deflect ownership. Learning how to take ownership is pivotal in your growth journey. When I started to realize that I am the one who chooses, that is when I realized the power I have. Otherwise, when we blame, we tend to victimize and feel sorry for ourselves. After all, it is so much easier to blame someone or something else and feel sorry for ourselves than it is to take ownership and put in the work to improve.

In order for you to turn your life around you must take back your power. In order to take back your power you must be willing to take 100 percent ownership in every area of your life. You can either make progress or make excuses;

but you cannot do both at the same time. For example, if you are late to work and your excuse is that there was traffic, the truth is you didn't plan well or allow time for traffic. You must own that you didn't make the right choices that get you to work on time and make a commitment to making better choices tomorrow.

If you aren't at your goal weight or fitness level, you might blame it on your busy schedule or that no one helps you with cooking meals. The reality is, we all have the ability to make healthier choices each and every day. Own where you are and identify the healthier choices you can start making today.

Maybe you are drowning in debt or, at the very least, not where you'd like to be financially. You might blame the divorce, inflation, your parents' relationship with money, etc. You might fall into the trap of victimizing and thinking there is no hope, then stop trying. Start with owning the role you played in getting yourself into your current situation. Then identify what steps you can take to create a financial position you are proud of.

One very important ingredient in being able to take ownership is self-awareness. Alert: if you were reading the last paragraph and thinking about how someone *else* needs this message, let's get the focus back on "self-awareness." It is about self-reflection and application, not trying to change or fix someone else. More than likely, the people who are not self-aware did not buy a book titled *Create Your Ideal Future* or anything related to personal development. So kudos to you for being self-aware enough to read this book! Now it is time to decide. It is time to *commit* to seeing this through.

Statistics show that about 40 percent of people never finish the books they start. And 98 percent of people who want to make a change in their lives never actually do it. They stop at the dreaming stage without ever acting on those dreams. Real change is not about when it's easy or feels right; it's about sticking with it no matter what.

I believe the reason people who desire change don't follow through is because they aren't clear on what they truly want or *how* they will get there. In this book, I will share with you tangible tools you can implement now to create the change you desire. These tools are simple, but the journey is not easy. Last I checked, Easy Street leads to nowhere. This book will challenge you while also helping you see that it is the small, simple things that make the biggest difference.

If you're ready to join me on this journey, let's commit to change together. Start by dedicating a bit of time each day to finish this book—even if it's just ten minutes. Let this commitment be a sign of a promise to yourself to transform your life from feeling stuck to soaring forward. Remember, commitment isn't about finding what works for now, it's about what works for a lifetime. Are you ready to stop just wondering about change and actually embrace it? Your decision will shape not just today but the rest of your life.

If you're ready to make this commitment, I want you to take it one step further and share that commitment with an accountability partner. Identify someone who has your best interest at heart and let them know that you are starting a new growth journey, with the first commitment being to finish this book by (insert date). Communicate with them what your consequence will be if you don't fulfill this commitment. Your consequence could be something like singing in public, wearing your rival team's jersey, paying them $100, you name it. This goal needs to have a specific deadline with a consequence if you don't follow through. Make sure the consequence drives you. Keep in mind that all of your choices, commitments, and actions have inherent consequences anyway. When you're intentional, that is where the magic happens. In the next chapter we will dive into some simple steps you can take to move closer to where you want to be in life. One step at a time.

Action Items

Secure an accountability partner to go on this growth journey with you. Go to my website (formpowerful-habits.com) to grab a free copy of my workbook to complete the "Making the Commitment" exercise from the "Taking Own-ership" chapter.

Be sure to communicate how your accountability partner can hold you accountable. For example, let them know you will be checking in with them daily by 5 p.m. If they don't receive an update, they can follow up with you the next morning by 10 a.m. Being specific about how you will be held accountable prevents you from feeling attacked and ensures they know how to help.

CHAPTER 2
The Power of Choice

By the end of this chapter, my hope is that you will grasp the power that you hold with your choices. Truly understanding the significance of choice is a massive step toward creating a life you are proud of. Ultimately, our lives are a result of our choices. If you don't like where your life is currently, make better choices. Both big and small.

If you think about it, you are making choices all day long. Some are as simple as deciding what to have for breakfast, while others, like choosing a career path, can be life-altering. At the time of the writing of this book, I find myself navigating through a challenging season of my life. After dedicating over fifteen years to a company I once believed I would serve indefinitely, circumstances have led me to an unexpected transition. The unfortunate exposure to the less desirable aspects of corporate America and fear-based management has been eye-opening.

However, amid these challenges, I have found strength and resilience through faith and courage. This transition has allowed me to deepen my reliance on prayer and make thoughtful decisions that will shape my future. I am convinced that on the other side of this discomfort lies a brighter and more fulfilling chapter. Maybe you, too, are faced with a personal or professional dilemma; or better yet, a pivotal moment that requires courage and a leap of faith.

This is where the importance of intentional living shines brightly. In my years of making deliberate decisions—choices as seemingly insignificant as resisting the snooze button or choosing a salad over a more indulgent meal—I have been training myself. Each of these decisions, small but deliberate, has built a solid foundation for facing moments like this with confidence. These everyday choices have strengthened my decision-making muscle, preparing me to handle life's bigger challenges with clarity and purpose.

My faith in God has also always been my steadfast guide through uncertainty, helping me navigate the path with hope and assurance. It reassures me that trusting in divine guidance is not only wise but also essential. As I stand on the brink of a major transition in life, leaving a job that no longer serves my soul, I am choosing to bet on myself. This isn't just about being brave; it's about having faith that there is a divine purpose for my life. I am ready for this moment, fortified by past decisions and guided by my faith.

Taking 100 Percent Ownership

In the last chapter, we talked about taking ownership for where we are in life. Now let's pause for a moment to reflect on how we got here. What choices have sculpted your path and might not be serving you as much as you'd hoped? Whether we are talking about relationships, spirituality, our mindset, or even our physical health, our choices carve out our reality. This can be applied to any area of your life.

Imagine feeling adrift in your relationship. The easy route is to point fingers, to place blame, and to wallow in victimhood. But what if, instead, you choose to be self-aware? You shift your gaze inward, recognizing your role and taking small steps toward reconnection. It's all about owning what's yours and breaking the spiral of negativity.

The same goes for our spiritual journey. If your relationship with God seems distant, retrace your steps to see what choices led you away. God's steadfast, He hasn't budged. It's you who must make the trek back, one choice at a time.

Fitness and health? Oh, how the excuses can flow! "Healthy eating's expensive!" we cry, while perhaps ignoring the pricey caffeine habit that doesn't exactly scream "healthy". Or we lament the scarcity of time for cooking, while generously spending hours scrolling through feeds. I realize how easily these poor choices can creep in and take hold. But remember, you have the power—a lot more than you give yourself credit for.

I want to take you through two exercises in this chapter to help you to get clear on where you want to be as well as take inventory of where you are currently. It is best to complete both exercises before moving on to the next chapter.

Create Your Ideal Future

In the spirit of making choices, one of the most important choices you can make is the type of life you want to live. That's right! You get to *choose*! How liberating!

I think it is worth noting here that I am deeply rooted in my faith and wholeheartedly believe in God's word. The scripture says, "'For I know the plans I have for you,' declares the Lord, 'plans to prosper you and not to harm you, plans to give you hope and a future'" (Jeremiah 29:11). This promise reassures me that God has a purpose for me, one that is filled with hope and prosperity. The Bible also says, "May He give you the desire of your heart and make all your plans succeed" (Psalms 20:4). I trust in His divine wisdom and creation, knowing that He has blessed me with the ability to shape my life. In this exercise, we will focus on gaining clarity about what you truly desire, using God's ultimate plan for your life as the foundational cornerstone. I believe that the deepest desires of your heart are intricately linked to your divine purpose, as all good things originate from Him.

I know this all sounds a bit cliché, but I fully believe we are creators! We have the power to *create* the life of our dreams. I find the most successful people in life are the ones who know what they want. They know where they are going. Once you know that, you can get clear on what types of choices you need to make. The people who know this don't just make the most money. They also have the most confidence and bring the most value to those around them.

Take some time today to get clear on what you want. The reality is, most people don't know what they want or where they are going. They are just going through the motions of life on autopilot. I believe the majority of people are living in a vicious cycle of mindless distraction, negative thoughts, and/or worry swirling in their minds with little to no focus on what they truly want. So today is your lucky day! You get to invest time and energy into one of the most important exercises you will ever do. This simple but powerful tool is a vital step that cannot be skipped. Take time to prayerfully and thoughtfully answer the following "ideal future" questions. Be sure to write down your answers with clarity **before moving on**:

1. What are three words to describe how you want to *feel* in your ideal future?
2. What are the unique gifts and talents you will be using in your ideal future to bring value to the world around you?

3. Where will you live? Be specific—describe your part of the world, your street, your home.
4. Who is important in your life? Some examples could include family, friends, clients, etc.
5. What does your perfect weekday look like? What would happen with your family, friends, work, or any other part of your life? The more detailed you can get, the better this exercise will work for you. I have included an example day in the accompanying workbook.
6. Describe your physical, spiritual, emotional, and financial health.
7. What kind of impact do you want to make on the world around you? Paint a very clear picture of what the ideal outcome looks like.

One more significant piece of wisdom to share: your identity has power because it guides your choices. If you see yourself as a successful, disciplined, and impactful individual, your choices will align accordingly. Conversely, if you cling to an old identity at odds with your aspirations, you might sabotage your efforts to change.

For example, if I identify as a loving mother who is in shape, well balanced, financially free, and making an impact on the community around me, I will start to make choices that fall in line with a multi-millionaire mom/wife/health-nut etc. On the contrary, if I still identify as the irresponsible unreliable party girl who thinks it would be pretty cool to be successful, no matter how hard I try, I will still subconsciously make decisions that the party girl would have made. Then I would get down on myself and say things like, "See! I'm never going to change!" or "Why am I like this?" When our identity is out of alignment with our choices, if our identity is strong enough, it will pull our choices back into alignment. So this is a very important step to take!

When you complete the "ideal future" exercise above, take note of the new identity you are taking on. Really let it resonate with you and create an image in your mind of you living your ideal future. The more you connect with where you want to go as if you're already there, you will step into your new identity and your choices will follow suit. We will get into this more later; for now, just complete Step 1 prior to moving on to Step 2.

Intentional Observation

Now that you are clear on what you want, it is time to take an inventory of the choices you are currently making. For the next twenty-four hours take note of the decisions you make, especially those that are habitual. Don't overthink it, just jot them down, you can use the sheet provided in the workbook or just make your own list. Which habits are moving you toward the life you desire, and which ones do you want to shift? The next twenty-four hours are purely for observation, intentional observation. Do not spiral into negativity, judging your habits and becoming overwhelmed by what you believe you are doing "wrong." Instead, have a little celebration when you identify which habits aren't moving you in the direction you want to go. After all, the goal is to choose better and make a change. We need to know which choices need to be rectified.

I hope I have your attention because this is very important. Again: *do not* let this discussion on choices overwhelm you. Take a breath. Some people look at the big picture and feel engulfed by its enormity, then give up. We are not looking to change everything at once. We will start small and build over time. Progress over perfection. Now I want to challenge you to put down this book and go into observation mode for the day. If it makes it easier, set an alarm on your phone for every waking hour. When the alarm goes off, take note of the choices you made within that hour. Pick back up tomorrow (put it on your calendar for tomorrow and do *not* skip tomorrow's reading) to continue this journey of transforming your choices and habits in order to lead a life of fulfillment and impact...one you can be proud of.

Action Items

Go to my website (formpowerfulhabits.com) to grab a free copy of my workbook to complete the "Create Your Ideal Future" exercise as well as the "Current Habits" exercise from the "The Power of Choice" chapter.

CHAPTER 3
Progress Over Perfection

Now that you know what your ideal future looks like, it's easy to think perfection is the aim. But really, growth and progress should always be our goal. My high school arrest was a huge turning point, but it wasn't like a magic switch that made my life choices perfect from that point forward. It was just the beginning of a path aimed at constant growth.

To me, pursuing growth is pursuing excellence, not perfection. Perfection and excellence, while often perceived as similar, differ significantly in their approach and impact. Perfection is the pursuit of a flawless state, where mistakes are not tolerated. It focuses on achieving an ideal end result, often emphasizing external standards and expectations. This pursuit is linked to a fixed mindset, where the fear of mistakes can overshadow growth, leading to stress and frustration. The pressure to be flawless can become overwhelming, making perfection a demotivating path. That is why many people give up on their pursuit of goals.

In stark contrast, excellence is about striving to do your best and to improve continuously. It focuses more on the process of growth and personal development rather than merely the end result. A key component of pursuing excellence is the concept of getting 1 percent better every day. This idea emphasizes that small, consistent improvements can lead to significant progress over time. By embracing each day—and moment—as an opportunity to learn and make wise choices, we gradually build toward greatness.

Excellence encourages a growth mindset, where failures become stepping stones toward advancement. It views challenges as opportunities to evolve, making the pursuit of excellence both motivating and sustainable. Rather than fearing mistakes, excellence emphasizes reaching your own potential through continuous, incremental improvements...one choice at a time. By focusing on being 1 percent better each day, the pursuit of excellence becomes a fulfilling and enriching journey, offering the beauty of learning and evolving, unlike the unattainable quest for perfection.

I believe the adage, "If you're not growing, you're dying." Each day (and even moment) should move us closer to being the best version of ourselves and creating our ideal future. In one of Ed Mylett's podcast episodes, he shares a story of a time that he took his son to the car wash and an older gentleman asked, "How old is your son?" Ed answered that he is six. The man said something to the effect of, "Enjoy your son now; when he's seven, the six-year-old you know will be gone forever." Ed replied respectfully, "Sir, at what age did that stop for you?" He was asking the man to reflect on at what point in his life did he stop growing and evolving. This is a great point of reflection for many adults. Do we think that once we reach a certain age we have arrived and are officially "adulting"?

Do we think that once we are out of school we no longer need to pursue learning? Many people in our society have fallen into this trap of complacency and, quite frankly, regression. I cannot imagine living a life in which I am not pursuing growth. I turned forty a couple of months ago and I intend to grow and evolve from my thirty-nine-year-old self. I will continue to create new habits, learn new skills, and develop more relationships.

Fast forward to when you reach the end of your life, which path did you take? The one where you were intentionally growing and evolving? Where you were showing up at your best and fully present, making each day mean something? Or did you take the path of unintentional reaction? Where life is tossing you around with the wind? Not actually achieving anything or impacting anyone? Do you just wake up one day and say, "How did I get here?" "What could I have done differently?"

One thing that has really helped me in living an intentional life of pursuing growth and excellence is to always have goals that I am striving to achieve. I actually cannot imagine living a life that isn't goal-oriented. Would it be like the movie *Groundhog Day*? Each day looks the same and we are just checking boxes and passing time? We are *not* here to pass time! We are here to make it count!

Early on in my journey of being goal-oriented, I became obsessive with each goal, making it a destination. I also tied some sense of relief to each goal. I would think things like, "Once I achieve X, I will *then* be able to Y." Y would sometimes be things like I am now able to afford to buy something, or I will be happier, less stressed, etc. What I have come to realize is that the goal is not the destination. Life does not get easier when you reach certain milestones, you get stronger.

It is not about what you accomplish, it is about who you become in the process. I believe that none of us were called to live a mediocre life, we are here to achieve God-sized dreams! We should all be shooting for things that require faith and growth. However, don't get caught up in the trap that once you arrive at your goal, life somehow gets easier or you will be ultimately fulfilled. Nothing replaces the peace that God provides. So chasing things of this world will not replace your spiritual well-being.

With that being said, the life of chasing and achieving goals is beyond rewarding and provides us an opportunity to grow and make a real impact on the world. I believe that complacency and mediocrity are tempting traps that work against us fulfilling our true purpose. Especially in a post-Covid environment, people have really gotten complacent. I find more and more people justifying mediocrity and masking it as priorities or self-care. Don't get me wrong, I believe Covid was a great reset for evaluating priorities, habits, and goals. However, don't confuse laziness with self-care. There's a time to rest and reflect, but there's also time to take action, and nothing happens without action.

Now that we are clear on what your ideal future looks like, let's set goals that keep us on a path to get there. In the accompanying workbook you will find a Goals Worksheet that helps you create and break down your goals. I believe that you always need to know the score in order to change the score. So keeping your goal-tracking in front of you is an important part of accomplishing them. Most people make the mistake of setting goals and then putting them away in a drawer. Only to find them a year later when cleaning out said drawer, realizing they didn't even take the first step. I want to encourage you to print the goal worksheet (one for each goal) and keep it in front of you every single day. That's right, 365 days per year. Living a life of intention doesn't happen once a week, it is a daily habit, a lifestyle.

One thing I have learned over time (especially in a career of sales) is that your goals should be so big they scare you! If your goals don't scare you (or at the bare minimum, give you that nervous feeling in your stomach), they are not big enough. Don't kid yourself into thinking a "safe" goal is somehow better for you. Like you are trying to prevent yourself from being disappointed. What you're really trying to do is stay inside your comfort zone. That is *not* where growth takes place. So first things first, set goals that scare you, push you, and will cause you to grow into a new person! Like I mentioned before, we don't achieve for the sake of achieving. The true reward of setting goals and achieving them is who you become in the process.

You also want to make sure that your goals are SMART (everyone knows this!): Specific, Measurable, Achievable (not average), Relevant, and Time-bound. Know clearly what you want to achieve, how you measure it, what achieving it looks like (really visualize this!), and make sure it is relevant to you…something that means something to you and is Time-bound. There needs to be a deadline. Otherwise, you can spend your whole life chasing one goal but never really measuring it to know if you're on track.

Throughout my career in sales, one of my favorite things I have learned is that limits truly only exist in your mind. If you think a goal is too big and you would never be able to achieve it, you're right! If you think you are more than capable, fully expect it to happen, and are willing to put in the effort to get there, it will be so! I learned a hack to quit thinking something was too big or out of reach, and that was to minimize its magnitude.

For example, I remember an early mentor telling me I need to have a minimum of $5,000 in the bank at all times. If my account starts to drop below $5K, I should start to worry. At the time I thought she was *insane*—I thought $5,000 was a ton of money! She told me to start by making $1,000 my minimum, with a short-term goal of it becoming a $5,000 floor in my bank account. Once I saw how my mind shifted around this one item in my life, I started applying it to other areas of life (and growing my floor amount in the bank). This changes your relationship with money and success. If you think a certain amount of money is a lot of money, more than likely you won't ever have it. But if you realize it is "only" $100,000, $500,000, etc., you start to expect yourself to be in that position financially. This applies to any goal you set for yourself, in all areas of your life.

As you set out to achieve your goals, be prepared to take on a world of distraction. Have you ever heard the expression, "If the devil can't make you sin, he'll make you busy"? We live in a world of complete distraction. So many things are competing for our attention: social media, busy schedules, work, kids, sports, Netflix, you name it. It is extremely easy to get distracted from your goals and most importantly, the daily habits needed to achieve them. Put a plan in place to overcome this. Being proactive is important to your success. We will dive more into some ways to overcome this later in the book. Here's your reminder to commit to finishing this book and process. Remember why you committed, what your consequence is for not finishing, and see it through to the end. You're doing great!

Action Item

In the spirit of getting 1 percent better, create two or three SMART goals that will move you closer to creating your ideal future. They can be personal, professional, spiritual, relational, etc. Go back and read your ideal future worksheet prior to setting these goals to ensure alignment with what you truly want—not necessarily what you think you *should* want.

Go to my website (formpowerfulhabits.com) to grab a free copy of my workbook to complete the "SMART Goals" exercise from the "Progress over Perfection" chapter.

CHAPTER 4
Choose Your Habits Wisely

When I was in high school, my friends often referred to me as "downward spiral" because of the poor choices I continued to make. It became a joke and, unfortunately, a part of my identity. Needless to say, I was not named "most likely to succeed" in the school yearbook. It is quite scary to think that I could have held on to that identity and ultimately lived an entirely different life. I firmly believe that God intervened so that I could fulfill my purpose of helping people choose a better life!

The key is to keep your ideal future front of mind and have 100 percent commitment to achieving it. There is a big difference in being *interested* in living a better life and being 100 percent *committed* to doing what it takes to get there. Giving up isn't an option. Once you have that level of commitment, the next step is to keep the promises you make to yourself. That is why it is important to start small with two or three new daily habits and build from there. Once you say you are going to make these choices daily, you must follow through. We all know people who are all talk, no action. Don't be that person. When you say you're going to do something, do it! The best way to make this shift is to tell your accountability partner what habits you are committing to for the next ninety days and have them consistently check in with you. Don't skip this part. People who don't want to be held accountable either don't have a clear vision of where they're going or they simply aren't committed.

Now that you have observed your current choices in the chapter 2 exercise, let's first celebrate the small wins. Even if your only healthy choice was making this observation, it is worth celebrating! Surely there were some choices you made that are moving you closer to where you want to be. If you made a choice of grilled chicken over fries or logging off early to get a restful night's sleep, acknowledge that victory. For the choices that are less than stellar like hitting the snooze button or mindlessly scrolling instead of taking action, notice them, own them, learn, and then gently let them go. Don't continue to replay the negative script. You've got a new scene today. A fresh start to make intentional choices that are moving you closer to where you want to be. And you're investing the time in evaluating your choices and habits, which is a huge step in creating the life you were meant to live.

Let's get clear on the daily choices you would like to start making that move you closer to your ideal future. Taking into account your ideal future, current habits, and SMART goals, make a list of the daily habits you would eventually like to have. You can use the accompanying workbook to create your list. Here are some examples to get you started:

Wake up at 5 a.m.
Read Bible
Prayer
Gratitude journal
Exercise
Healthy breakfast/shake
Positive affirmations
Meditation/visualization
Send encouraging message to three people
Drink one gallon of water
Do something uncomfortable
Plan tomorrow (with great detail)
Two hours with kids (no screens)
Learn something new
Review goals before bed
Sleep by 9:30 p.m.

When I had my turning point, I didn't make *any* of the choices listed above. Today, almost every item listed is a daily habit for me. I hope my story will encourage you to know that I was on a path of complete destruction heading nowhere, and now I am consistently choosing healthy habits in order to show up as the best version of myself.

One foundational and extremely impactful habit I have formed is a positive and intentional morning routine. My morning routine has grown over the years, as many of the items listed I complete in the morning before the rest of my family wakes up. Imagine this type of routine: in the evening you get lost in mindless scrolling to eventually look at the time and realize you need to go to sleep. You start calculating how many hours of sleep you will get and what is the latest possible minute you can wake up in order to be on time for your first appointment. In the morning your alarm goes off way too soon, you subconsciously hit the snooze button a few times. Then, realizing what time it is, you frantically jump out of bed to rush around getting ready to run out the door. You're running behind and not only is there traffic, but everyone else on the road has forgotten how to drive, except you, of course. You're late and tell your coworkers it was due to traffic, taking no ownership of the fact that you didn't leave the house early enough to account for rush hour traffic. You then do your best to put on your positive pants and give a good effort at work while running on fumes and maybe some coffee. Does that sound familiar? I know this routine all too well, as I used to live it!

When our day starts off chaotic, odds are the rest of the day will follow suit. When we start the day with a positive mindset and a full cup, we are prepared to meet the day's challenges and create with intention versus react to circumstances. Just as the flight attendant instructs you to first put on your own face mask, you can't pour from an empty cup. Even if you start with waking up fifteen minutes earlier than normal and filling your cup (not turning to social media) before starting your day. This produces exponential results in how you show up.

Once you have completed your list of new daily habits, pick two or three you will implement daily for the next ninety days. You might have days where you mess up, but don't let that get in the way of continuing this journey and trying again. This isn't about radical changes overnight; it's about intentional, mindful steps—stepping stones to the habits that support our dreams. Start small to build your confidence. For example, if you currently wake up at 8 a.m., joining the 5 a.m. club may not be a wise first step. The point in picking only two or three new habits early on is to build your self-confidence by keeping the promises you make yourself. This will ultimately help shape your new identity.

As you finalize your first two or three daily choices you're going to commit to, I would encourage you to listen to your gut. Where do you believe you should start? What will have the biggest impact and also be something you will stick with? If you are still drawing a blank on where to start, I would recommend you to start with prayer, exercise, and planning your tomorrow. Here is some insight on each if you choose to start here:

Prayer

For me, intentional time with God in the morning before I start my day puts everything into perspective. Matthew 6:33-34 are some of my favorite Bible verses that have always held true in my life. It says, "Seek first His kingdom and His righteousness, and all these things will be given to you as well. Therefore, do not worry about tomorrow, for tomorrow will worry about itself. Each day has enough trouble of its own." If you notice, the verse doesn't say seek Him when it's convenient or whenever you think about it. It says seek *first*. You don't have to be a Bible scholar or super spiritual leader to spend time in prayer each morning.

If you find yourself not knowing what to pray about, refer to Philippians 4:6 which says, "Do not be anxious about anything, but in every situation, by prayer and petition, with thanksgiving, present your requests to God." In other words, nothing is off the table. Whatever you might be worried about, give it to God.

It is about relationship, not religion. So don't overthink it. Just have an honest conversation with God each morning.

When I fall out of rhythm with my morning prayer time, I notice I start to shift to being more internally focused. If we're not careful, we will naturally begin to think the world revolves around us and our problems and lose sight of the eternal value of our daily choices. As a type A striver, I could easily fall into the trap of chasing worldly success without any kingdom impact. I find that my morning time with God helps me keep an eternal perspective and approach the day with the intention to love and serve others.

Exercise

Exercise is one of the best ways to build self-confidence. And I'm not only talking about confidence in your appearance. I am referring to the confidence that comes from keeping the promises you make to yourself. Working out tends to be an area in which many people struggle with follow-through. Yet no one ever regrets a workout. Exercise has many health benefits including the release of endorphins, which are a natural brain chemical that can improve your sense of well-being. It is a natural boost that creates momentum with more healthy choices throughout your day.

If you are not someone who exercises daily, I would set a goal to move your body in some way every day. It could be a ten-minute walk, squats while you brush your teeth or doing a plank contest with your kids. Start small and work your way up to forty-five-plus minutes and 7,000-plus steps per day. You will notice drastic improvements in several areas of your life when you fully commit to this habit.

Maybe you have struggled with consistency in exercising several times in the past and are wondering what will make this time different. You now have a newly formed identity that you are aligning your habits with. You also have an accountability partner who is on this journey with you. Remember there is a difference between being interested and being committed.

Planning Your Tomorrow

Nothing really gets done unless I write it down. I have been writing out my plan for tomorrow every day for over fifteen years. I once had a mentor tell me, "Your day is not over until your tomorrow is planned." There is something really powerful in writing out a plan as you are visualizing a successful day before it happens. It is important to write down your goals and habits, then keep your plan in front of you as you move through your day. When I am adding in new daily habits I want to form, I add them to my daily plan. That has been a process that has really worked for me.

Action Item

Go to my website (formpowerfulhabits.com) to grab a free copy of my workbook to complete the "New/Future Daily Habits" exercise from the "Choose Your Habits Wisely" chapter. Highlight the two or three new daily choices that you will be starting with and share them with your accountability partner.

CHAPTER 5
Consistency is Key

Congratulations on making it to chapter 5! Truly celebrate how far you have come. At this point you have:

- ✓ Solidified an accountability partner who will hold you to completing this book by your given deadline. Said accountability partner knows your consequence if you happen to fall short (which you won't 😊).
- ✓ Clarified your ideal future.
- ✓ Spent twenty-four hours observing your current/old habits.
- ✓ Completed your Goals Worksheet for two or three goals that move you closer to your ideal future.
- ✓ Identified which daily habits will help you achieve your goals and create your ideal future.

Wow! That is so much progress! You are significantly further ahead than the majority of people...even strivers who have a strong desire to succeed but don't know where to begin.

You now know what choices you want to start making daily in order to show up as the best version of yourself and live a life you are proud of. Now that you know what you want and how to get there, *consistency* is the key to your success. As you consistently hold true to your commitment to these choices, you will notice the growth that takes place.

First, you will build trust within yourself. You start noticing that you are reliable in making good decisions. As you consistently make choices that reflect your true intentions, you start to see yourself as reliable and capable. This self-reliance is empowering; knowing that you can depend on yourself to make sound decisions builds a solid foundation.

You will also build your decision-making muscle, making it stronger and stronger. The more consistently you make good choices, the more good choices you begin to make. It is a ripple effect. Just like going to the gym, the more you show up and exercise, the stronger you get. Each positive choice reinforces your capability to make the next good decision, creating momentum around making good choices. And, as mentioned previously, your life is a result of your choices!

When I first made the decision to turn my life around, I was in a place where no one trusted me and I, frankly, didn't even trust myself. However, I knew the desire that I had to be successful and get my life on track. So I channeled that desire (which is something only you can do for yourself) into my actions. My starting place was *consistent follow-through*. I made it a point to always do what I said I would do, even if no one else knew about it. For example, if I say I am going to do laundry tomorrow, come hail or high water, I am doing laundry. Even if I didn't tell anyone else that I am committing to laundry, a haircut, paying bills, etc., I had to make sure I was forming the habit of following through.

This is where self-awareness and self-accountability come into play. You are the one who knows what you commit to and what you procrastinate. You know if you are making an excuse or making progress. If you are truly committed to growth, you have to be real with yourself. Instead of trying to appear perfect in the eyes of others, concern yourself with keeping the promises you make to yourself.

You might not need to completely transform every aspect of your life to see significant improvements. Perhaps you have a flourishing career, yet your personal relationships or health are not receiving the attention they deserve. Conversely, you might be thriving in your personal life but embarking on a new business venture where your habits will greatly influence your success. There could be just a few key areas where adopting new habits could dramatically change how you show up in life. Even if those around you aren't aware of the habits you wish to change, you know they might be holding you back. Whether you feel the need to make several changes or just a few, our focus will be on consistency in order to get 1 percent better every day.

The idea of improving just 1 percent each day may seem modest at first glance, but it's a profoundly powerful concept when looked at through the lens of consistency and compounding growth. Consistency is the magical element that magnifies these incremental gains, transforming them into substantial progress over time. By focusing on small daily improvements, you set the stage for exponential growth and development.

Moreover, the psychological benefits of focusing on 1 percent daily improvements are remarkable. It reduces the pressure of achieving drastic transformations overnight, making your goals more approachable and less daunting. As you celebrate these small victories, your confidence and motivation are boosted, encouraging you to continue striving toward creating successful habits that lead to your ideal future.

If you tend to be an all-or-nothing type of person, it is vitally important that you start small and build from there. Some people have a tendency to give up on everything altogether after one mishap, telling themselves they will try again "another day." You make decisions by the moment. So this is a moment-by-moment feat, one poor moment does not have to break your momentum and lead to a bad day...unless you allow it to.

In my experience, when you start the day strong you set yourself up for a successful day. However, things don't always go as planned. For example, let's say your first three new daily habits are to wake up at 5 a.m., exercise for forty-five minutes and pray for five minutes. You unknowingly snooze your alarm, wake up late, missing your morning workout and prayer time. You now are faced with another choice. While you can't turn back time to wake up earlier that day, you can make better choices for the remainder of the day that support those habits you committed to. Look at your calendar early in the day and schedule your workout and prayer time. *Create* time for these activities. Where there's a will, there's a way. So if you want to find the time for something, you will.

Another thing to strongly consider that day would be positioning yourself for a win in waking up early the following day. Here are some suggestions:

- Have a strong bedtime routine with a specific time goal for when to be asleep.
- Don't scroll your phone in bed.
- Have an alarm set across the room, requiring you to get out of bed to turn it off. Or you can download an app that requires you to complete math problems in order to turn off your alarm in the morning. This prevents oversleeping.

In this example, you have an opportunity to create solutions or make excuses. It is entirely up to you. Instead of focusing on what you did "wrong," give yourself grace and move on to the next moment and next best choice. The more you do this consistently, the sooner you will be able to show up as the best version of yourself.

My kids have the perfect opportunity to learn this concept through playing baseball. Their coaches are always telling them that the most important pitch is the next one. I absolutely love that my kids get to learn valuable lessons through sports. They are learning the importance of being able to move on quickly when experiencing a setback. You don't shy away from your goal, you reset and make the most of the next moment.

The same holds true in life. You will inevitably encounter resistance as you embark on this growth journey. Various challenges, like those highlighted in the earlier example, will test your consistency and present opportunities to either give yourself an "out" for the day or choose to make the best decisions possible for the rest of the day. The key lies in being deeply committed and aligned with your new identity, enabling you to persevere with your new habits. Over time, as you consistently reinforce these habits, they will become embedded in your subconscious mind, reducing the effort and resistance required to maintain them.

In the spirit of consistency, use the Habit Tracker in the accompanying workbook. Print that page to keep with you daily as you track your progress. You can also set reminders in your phone for each habit. Every day may not be perfect, but this tracker will help you to keep your intentional choices in front of you as well as see the wins and momentum you're creating. Focus on finding the progress, not perfection. Start with the two or three new daily habits you decided to form in chapter 4 and then build on them every ninety days (unless you feel ready to add on sooner). Remember, starting small and feeling momentum will keep you in the game of growth. If you find yourself feeling overwhelmed or falling short, scale back to one or two new habits. The goal initially is consistency and growth.

Action Item

Go to my website (formpowerfulhabits.com) to grab a free copy of my workbook to complete the "Habit Tracker" from the "Consistency is Key" chapter. You can also find an extra Habit Tracker file on the website so you can print them weekly. Keep it with you and track your progress daily.

Text your accountability partner daily to confirm that you followed through on your commitments. I recommend texting a picture of your completed daily habit tracker found in the workbook. Once these choices become habitual, you will add on two or three additional daily habits that move you closer to your ideal future, and repeat this process. In order to stay consistent, be sure to continue with your accountability partner as you layer more new habits.

CHAPTER 6
Mindset Matters

Garbage In, Garbage Out

Our minds are constantly consuming and recycling information. You may have heard the expression "garbage in, garbage out." This point was proven when I made the conscious decision to stop watching the news. It is no secret that the media thrives on viewership, and fear is ultimately what sells. I noticed a long time ago that watching the news was stealing my joy and planting seeds of fear in my mind.

The last time I watched the news was the night that I could not fall asleep because I was convinced that North Korea had a missile pointed directly at my house. Needless to say, that never happened. And if it had, there would have been absolutely nothing I could have done about it. So staying up and worrying does not serve me or anyone.

Similarly, I stopped watching scary movies over fifteen years ago. I found myself replaying scenes of movies filled with fear of things that will likely never happen. Now, I am not saying cut yourself off from entertainment, unless you find it to be necessary. Be aware of how your mind is impacted by what you are consuming. I do believe our day-to-day lives give us plenty of opportunities to avoid negativity, and we shouldn't go out of our way to consume more of it.

Being intentional with maintaining a positive mindset is more important now than ever before. At every moment in the day, we are given opportunities to choose our mindset. Ask yourself, "Am I proactively creating and focusing on what I want in life? Or am I merely reacting to uncontrollable circumstances and allowing them to consume my energy?"

For instance, one day, Jason arrived home visibly agitated after a long drive. He couldn't shake off the anger from an encounter with an aggressive driver on the highway. The other driver had cut him off so abruptly that Jason had to swerve to avoid a collision. For the rest of the day, Jason recounted the incident to everyone he spoke to—his family, his coworkers, his neighbor, even the delivery person. Each time he relived the story, his anger seemed to intensify.

It was as if the story was too heavy to carry alone, and sharing it somehow helped. But did it really? Every time he repeated the story, it was like he was adding another log to the fire of his frustration. By the end of the day, not only was the story much more dramatic than what actually happened, but all he could focus on was how reckless and inconsiderate drivers on the road could be. Not to mention how much time was wasted for Jason and each person he shared this story with.

Have you ever handled something similarly to Jason? A rude or reckless driver is just one minor example. Maybe you've had a meeting or event not go as planned. Or someone at work said something offensive that is now living rent free in your head. There are things that can very justifiably frustrate you and cause you to complain or even whine. How you handle these moments are crucial to your success in life.

Have you ever heard the concept, if you get a flat tire, are you going to slash your other three tires and call it a day? You get the premise, right? When something doesn't go your way, you have to be very intentional about not allowing that thing to bleed into many other parts of your day. We all tend to fester, complain, and replay negativity (looking for that validation of our feelings). I believe that most people want to be able to snap out of negative thoughts and don't know how. They believe saying things like "not today, Satan" or "positive vibes only" will do the job. Yet five minutes after making that declaration, their mind goes back to ruminating on the negativity they're trying to avoid. In my experience, we need to *take action* to shift our thoughts to positivity.

Is this something I can control?

When you find yourself ruminating, first ask yourself if this is something you can control. If it is, identify what needs to be done to resolve the issue and take action. If you're like most people, many of the items that you've allowed to live rent free in your head are uncontrollables. In my experience, if it is something that I cannot control, it is usually a complete waste of time and energy to focus on it. When you can learn to shift your focus and energy to the things you can control, you regain so much power to create a life you are proud of.

How many minutes will I live in this moment?

Next, I will ask myself how many minutes am I choosing to live in this moment. The true power is found in recognizing that it is a choice! I once had someone ask me, "Ashley, how do you stop yourself from thinking?" The answer is that I don't. I just redirect my thoughts, sometimes over and over. When I ask myself the above question, I will set a timer, most of the time for five minutes unless it's something really big. I think it's worth noting that if you are going through something significant like the loss of a loved one, job, or relationship, obviously that will take longer than five minutes to move past. However, you may need to complete this exercise several times each day, gradually spending fewer minutes consumed by the issue. Outside of significant loss, this exercise works extremely well for the majority of challenges we face in life.

During the five minutes (or time allotted), I can call someone, but the goal should be to limit it to one person. Choose this one person wisely. When we are feeling frustrated or angry, we are often tempted to call someone who will validate our feelings and pour fuel all over the fire. They are likely the friend who believes you could never do anything wrong. They may even pile on additional reasons why you should be upset and the world sucks. After all, misery does love company. Odds are someone came to mind when reading that example. Don't call that person. Choose wise counsel who will listen, empathize, and be solution-oriented. You may even want to proactively identify who your one phone call will be and make them aware of this exercise.

Don't call ten different people to poke holes in their boat for the sake of having an "OMG guess what" moment. Like Paul Molitor says, "Complaining is like vomiting. You might feel better after you get it out, but you make everybody around you sick." In that five minutes you can vent, feel what you feel, you don't need to suppress your feelings, just don't give them more fuel to grow with negativity.

Changing the channel

After you acknowledge and express your feelings once and the timer ends, it's time to change the channel. Remember that simply deciding to be positive doesn't necessarily mean your mind will shift to positive thoughts. In my experience, I need to take an actionable step that will help me to mentally change the channel.

Some actionable items that have worked for me include prayer, reading, speaking affirmations, meditation, listening to a song or a podcast, etc. In the accompanying workbook I have included a list of suggestions that can help you with redirecting your thoughts, which will ultimately redirect your energy, choices, and effort. The point in taking these steps is to shift your focus back to seeing the good and spending more energy on what you do want versus what you don't want. It will also be helpful to review your goals and visualize your ideal future each time you are changing the channel.

Years ago, I took a course by The Pacific Institute called Thought Patterns for High Performers. This was a pivotal course for me for many reasons. One being the lesson on how our thoughts and words matter. One of the exercises they challenge their students to do consists of wearing a rubber band on their wrist and any time they catch themselves saying or thinking negatively they snap the band on their wrist to "snap out of it." The first exercise is to go twenty-four hours without saying or even thinking anything negative. No complaining, gossiping, wallowing, or limiting thoughts. If one arises, you snap the rubber band and redirect your thinking. You could also implement this exercise (instead of the five-minute timer) prior to taking an actionable step to changing your mental channel.

Don't wait for issues to arise

> *"Life is 10 percent what happens to you
> and 90 percent how you respond to it."*
> **— Charles Swindoll**

Having a strong morning routine has been instrumental in my ability to handle what the day throws at me. It also allows me to show up as the best version of myself, for myself and everyone else. In order to fuel my mind, my morning routine always consists of prayer, meditation, reading, and positive affirmations. I have noticed that when I am intentional about consuming positivity (especially early in the morning), it has a dramatic effect on my entire day. Before these practices were a part of my morning routine, I was much more reactive, fragile, victimizing, and critical (especially of myself). I would focus on my flaws and where I fell short. This intentional practice of creating a positive mindset in the morning has changed everything for me.

Instead of focusing on avoiding negativity, I find it best to look for ways to consume positivity. It is almost like you are putting on your mental armor to show up prepared to respond to life's challenges as the victorious overcomer that you already are!

Action Item

Go to my website (formpowerfulhabits.com) to grab a free copy of my workbook to complete the "Changing the Channel in Your Mind" exercise from the "Mindset Matters" chapter. Read through the examples provided and consider what works best for you. Select one or two that resonate with you and keep them readily available to use when needed.

CHAPTER 7
Watch Your Words

My theme song in life is "Speak Life" by Toby Mac. If you've never listened to it, I highly recommend it! Pay close attention to the lyrics as they are both inspiring and impactful. This song resonates with me because my life experiences continue to prove the validity of every word. Change your words and you can change your world.

Start with Self-Talk

Early in my journey of growth and personal development, I learned that the words I say have a lot of power. I read that if you don't want something to be true about yourself, don't keep saying it. Those words really stuck with me, not just for myself, but for others I talk to as well.

Think about it like this: If you always talk about what you don't want to be, you end up becoming more like that. Where your focus goes, your energy flows. If you are continually focusing on what you don't want, you are going to get more of that. One of my biggest pet peeves is when people say "just my luck" when something doesn't go their way.

It's almost like they're manifesting things not to work in their favor and then affirming that things should continue not to work out for them. Another example is saying things like "I'm always late" or "I'm never motivated," your subconscious mind goes to work to prove that you are right. It's like your words are shaping who you are, even if you don't really mean for that to happen. It is a self-fulfilling prophecy.

We all know this, even if we don't think about it all the time. You know when you're worried and you don't even want to say what you're scared will happen? For example, you're lying awake at night and your mind is racing straight to a worst-case scenario involving a loved one's safety, you don't even want to speak that scenario out loud. That's because deep down, you know words have power.

Now, this isn't just for the big stuff. Even for small things like saying, "I'm not a reader" or "I'll always be in debt," our words have impact. Why would I keep saying things I don't want to be true? Instead, I learned to focus on what I want to become, not on what I'm trying to avoid.

In the beginning, I used to say not-so-great things about myself to explain away bad choices or things I didn't like about myself. Things I'd never say to someone else! But I realized I was downplaying my own abilities. I figured out that we need to take charge of our words and say positive things, ones that help us grow.

One of the best tools I found on my journey was using positive self-talk through daily affir-mations. I discovered this a bit later but wish I had started sooner. Simple changes in what you say can pave the way for the life you truly want.

Our minds have about 70,000 thoughts a day, and the majority are negative and repetitive. By practicing positive affirmations, you can change the way you think. It's like pulling weeds from a garden so the flowers—the positive thoughts—have room to grow.

Here's a good exercise for you to complete: Pay attention to what you say about yourself for a whole day. Whether you say it out loud or just think it, write these thoughts down. You can use the "Speak Life" worksheet in the accompanying workbook. For the next twenty-four hours, write down all the negative self-talk that runs through your mind. Make sure you are looking through the lens of your new identity that aligns with your ideal future. Odds are, you have limiting beliefs that will hold you back from reaching your destiny. For example, you might say or believe "I am never going to be financially free" or "I am just not consistent." Maybe you're not that blunt with yourself and you say things like "I wish I was consistent" or "I wish I was debt-free." These statements and beliefs keep you focused on what you aren't and what you don't have. The point in this exercise is to shift your identity in a more intentional and consistent way.

Just like the observation around daily choices, don't overthink it, just jot down your negative self-talk. Specifically, what are you saying and/or believing about yourself that isn't moving you closer to your ideal future? The next twenty-four hours are purely for observation, intentional observation. Do not spiral into negativity judging yourself and becoming overwhelmed by what you believe you are doing "wrong." Instead, celebrate when you identify which beliefs aren't moving you in the direction you want to go. Remember, the goal is to choose better and make a change.

Once you have completed the list of negative self-talk, the next step is to create positive statements to replace them. For instance, instead of saying "I'm always late," you could say, "I am proud to be early for my appointments." And instead of "I will always be overweight," you can start saying, "I am healthy and energized at my ideal weight." If this is a new practice for you, it can feel uncomfortable or inauthentic. It's important to note, if you don't do this step, you're naturally focusing on what you don't want...and you'll get more of that. In order to redirect your thoughts, you have to offset your default negativity and worry. The reason it's uncomfortable is because it requires growth and intention. If you feel like you are repeating a lie to yourself, that's okay. It's part of reprogramming your subconscious mind and teaching it the way you would like it to think. The more you affirm what you want to be true, the more you think, speak, and act the part.

To get you started, here are a few ground rules. Focus on the three P's:

1. Positive

Being intentionally positive is a must. Avoid words like "not," "don't," and "won't." Instead of saying "I will not spend money," try "I am wise with money I earn." The goal is to offset this default negative way of thinking.

2. Personal

Choose affirmations that are right for you. It has to be what *you* really want. Not what someone else wants for you or what you think you are supposed to want. They must be personal. You can only affirm for yourself, not for your spouse, kids, coworkers, or friends. Most importantly, always ensure your affirmations align with your ideal future and what you believe God has in store for your life.

3. Present Tense

If you speak it as though it's already happening, you will start making choices that align with that belief. When speaking affirmations, you want to speak as though it is already so, not something you will "one day" have in the future For example, "I will one day be debt free." Speaking this statement daily will always keep this desire out of reach. Rather, speak into existence that "I am proud to be living a wealthy and debt-free life." If you speak it as though it's already happening, you will start making choices that align with that belief. Over time, notice how this begins to shift you toward your new identity.

Here are some examples of affirmations:

I am abundantly blessed and highly favored.
I am anointed and guided by the Holy Spirit.
I choose to be full of joy, love, and gratitude.
I am eagerly looking for ways to serve others.
My high vibrations manifest my desires.
My life is filled with miracles.
I naturally find the good in every situation.
I am proud to be a great wife and mom.
I am grateful that everything is always working out for me.
I am an impactful woman of discipline and consistency.
The older I get, the healthier I become.
I enjoy eating healthy foods that fuel my body.
I am proud to be in the best shape of my life.
I am grateful to be financially free and living generously.

Create eight to ten daily affirmations that you believe serve you most. You can always build on from there. You can use the accompanying workbook to list your affirmations. Take the time to write these out (do not skip this step). The key is to start talking to yourself instead of listening to yourself. The weeds grow naturally in the garden, so if we are only listening to ourselves, odds are, it is going to be more negative than positive. Use this exercise to start talking to yourself in a kinder way. When you hear negative self-talk in your head, replace it with something positive. It sounds weird, right? But talking to yourself in this positive way gives you power. Your words help create your life, and it's up to you to shape it beautifully.

In order to make this a habit, I recommend that you say your positive affirmations *out loud* every single morning and evening. You could also record yourself saying your affirmations and listen to them at night before you fall asleep. There are studies that show your brain reaches a "theta" state before falling asleep. This is the best stage to access your subconscious mind and tell it what you want it to believe. Pause after speaking each affirmation and really visualize the experience, emotion, and feeling associated with that new belief. This detail will shift your identity as you become more familiar and comfortable in the new reality you are affirming. By visualizing and feeling each affirmation as if it is already so, you are learning how to feel, walk, and act in your new reality. The more frequently you do this, the more comfortable you become, which will in turn shape your new identity and future habits. At minimum, you need to speak them out loud every day.

When you make the very impactful and intentional choice to focus on what you want, both when you wake up and when you go to bed, you'll be well on your way to living the life you dream about, the life you deserve.

Action Item

Go to my website (formpowerfulhabits.com) to grab a free copy of my workbook to complete the "Speak Life" exercise from the "Watch Your Words" chapter.

CHAPTER 8
Believing in Yourself

Do you believe you are worthy of living a successful life? Do you believe you are capable of making the necessary changes to live a life you are proud of? Has anyone ever made you feel unworthy or inadequate? There are different components that go into fully believing in yourself, and I want to equip you to go on this journey with increasing belief in yourself.

In order to understand ourselves better, it's important to know the differences between self-worth, self-confidence, and self-esteem. These are like different pieces of a puzzle that show how we see and value ourselves. They all play a big role in your growth journey and how well you will stick with your new habits. Let's learn what each of them means, how we can improve them, and how self-sabotage can get in the way of our growth.

Self-worth is about realizing that you are valuable just because you exist. Ephesians 2:10 says, "For we are God's handiwork, created in Christ Jesus to do good works, which God prepared in advance for us to do." It doesn't matter how well you do in school, how much money you have in the bank or how many friends you have; your worth is about knowing you are important and special just by being you. That means your self-worth is not something you earn. It is your birthright!

Let me say it louder for the people in the back...you are not earning your worth! You are already worthy. Other people's opinions of you have zero bearing on your value. I believe that God has placed a special calling on your life that is unique to you. Let that really sink in! The world needs you to be the person *you* were created to be. The world doesn't need you to be like someone else and the world certainly doesn't need you to lay low and play small. You were bought at a high price and that value already exists in God's own image. You just need to realize, own, and walk in that worth. Exude the confidence that you are here for a reason and the world is better because you're in it!

If you find yourself tying your self-worth to other people's opinions of you, it is time to flip that script. Have you ever had an experience in a social setting when you said or did something that was embarrassing in the moment? Then, after you leave and the event is long over, you are still repeating the situation in your mind wondering what people are thinking about you. You're thinking thoughts like "Maybe I offended them," or "They probably think I am so _____." You can fill in the blank with your label of choice:

dumb, weird, crazy, etc. Odds are that not one single person is replaying that same scenario in their minds after it passed. They are more than likely replaying their own scenario, concerning themselves with other people's opinions of them. Most people are thinking about themselves, not you. The best thing you can do when you start to worry about what others think about you is to:

1. Remind yourself that more than likely, they are not even thinking about you.
2. Assume they are for you and not against you. This trick has worked so well for me over the years. If you catch yourself wondering what others think, assume they are for you and move on. It really doesn't require any more time or attention than that quick decision.
3. Remind yourself who you are! I am a child of God living out His purpose in my life. Every time I succumb to self-doubt worrying about what others think, I am distracted from my destiny. You can't control other people, but you can control what you allow yourself to believe and focus on.

Self-confidence is the belief that you can do things well and handle different challenges. It's like knowing you can ride a bike or speak in front of the class without fear. If you look back on the challenges you have already overcome in life, that alone should boost your self-confidence. I view self-confidence like self-trust. Do I trust myself to be able to do this, handle this, or achieve this?

Self-confidence comes from keeping the promises you make to yourself. After I was arrested, life got really tough. My family didn't trust me anymore. They weren't sure if I would make the right choices or even tell the truth about my actions. I had turned into someone I didn't want to be, and they saw it too.

Maybe you're in the same place. You've decided, "I am changing. I am going to be a new person and create a new life." But it's hard when no one believes you. You might find yourself thinking a lot about how to make them trust and believe you. But what worked for me was different.

I realized I first needed to trust myself before I worried about my family or anyone else trusting me. I had to be sure I wouldn't mess things up again. I needed to keep my promises to myself and do the things I said I would.

As mentioned when we discussed consistency, that is where my journey began. Each promise I made, I had to keep it, no matter what. Before my arrest, I didn't care much about keeping promises or making good choices. I would joke about it and say self-deprecating comments like, "Oh yeah, that's just like me!" as if it was funny. I would laugh it off pretending to be carefree. But the truth was, every time I didn't do what I said I would, I lost a bit of confidence in myself. Once I decided that I didn't want to be that person anymore, I knew I had to start putting more weight on the decisions I was making, both big and small.

I started with small tasks. If I said I would call my grandma (affectionately known as "Nanny") the next day, I had to do it. It didn't matter if it was a secret promise that I never shared with anyone. I followed through on my commitments, earning my own trust, bit by bit. Before anyone else believed in me, I did.

Now I have a ton of confidence in myself. If I promise to do something, I know that outside of uncontrollable circumstances, I will get it done.

As an example, I recently made a commitment to post daily on LinkedIn in order to bring value and grow my network. At the time of the commitment, this was something that was new and extremely uncomfortable for me. I had not historically been someone that posted on social media very much at all. However, when I made the commitment, I had extreme confidence that I would follow through.

And at the time of writing this, I am still posting daily. I'm confident that at the time of publishing this book, I will still be posting and I will be even better at it.

I am now at a point where when I want to make a shift in my life or push myself outside of my comfort zone, I identify what habits I need to form and then have complete trust in myself to follow through. I put those habits on my daily plan and take action on what I committed to do each day.

The goal is for you to form that confidence of knowing you will follow through on your commitments. You can't get that confidence from anyone else. You don't need others to believe in you first. You form that belief in yourself and it all starts with taking action and following through on your word.

Self-esteem is how you feel about yourself overall, like how much you like and respect yourself. It's about looking in the mirror and thinking, "I am good at things and I like who I am." To improve your self-esteem, try talking to yourself kindly. You just completed a list of daily affirmations that will help you talk to yourself more and listen to yourself less. Sticking to your daily positive affirmations will significantly help you boost your self-esteem. The key, as with anything, is consistency. Focus on things you do well, no matter how small. If you want to intentionally do a better job of focusing on the things you do well, start a What Went Well journal that you write in at the end of every day. Spend as little as two minutes journaling things you did well that day. Nothing negative, only the positives. This exercise strengthens the muscle that looks for the good. Another way to boost self-esteem is to set goals that you can reach and celebrate when you achieve them. You already created two or three SMART goals in chapter 3. Stick with the daily habits that keep you on track to achieve these goals knowing these actions will inevitably build your self-esteem. Finally, being around people who support and care for you also helps in feeling good about yourself. More to come on this in the next chapter.

Self-Sabotage: Have you ever set a goal and found it hard to achieve, even when you *really* wanted it? This might be because of something called self-sabotage. Self-sabotage happens when people, often without realizing it, get in the way of their own success. This can happen because of the beliefs we have about what we deserve or what we think we're capable of achieving.

All I wanted for my fortieth birthday was a golf cart. Do I play golf? No. Live in a golf course community? Nope. But we do live in Florida and are able to drive it on the nearby roads in our community. My husband thought this was a completely unnecessary purchase and at first said I needed to think of something else for my birthday. Sticking to my guns, I told him that a golf cart was the only thing I wanted. Being the supportive and generous husband he is, he conceded and got the golf cart. Might I point out that he absolutely loves this golf cart and uses it all the time! Once we started driving it around town, we realized that the governor—the device used to control the speed of the cart—is set to 25 mph. So no matter how hard we press the gas, or even when driving downhill, this golf cart will not go faster than 25 mph.

Now, let's think about how this concept relates to self-sabotage in our lives. Imagine your goals and ambitions are like driving a golf cart toward a destination. The governor in our minds consists of the beliefs and limits we set for ourselves. If you believe you can't go beyond a certain level in terms of achievements or self-worth, this mental governor will kick in, much like the one in our golf cart.

For instance, if you think you can only reach a certain level of success, like earning a specific amount of money or achieving a certain fitness goal, your "mental governor" might subconsciously hold you back from pushing beyond those limits. Even if you want to succeed more, just like trying to drive faster, these deep-seated beliefs can keep you from going the distance.

Imagine a person who believes they can never earn more than $50,000 a year. This belief acts like a "governor" on their potential. They work hard to reach this $50,000 mark because it matches their internal expectation of what they deserve. Even if they dream about making more, like $100,000 a year, their actions might not reflect this desire.

This is because, beyond the $50,000 mark, subconscious self-sabotage can kick in. Without realizing it, they might start making choices that prevent them from earning more or advancing financially. For example, they might find excuses to skip work, or make financial decisions that lead to unnecessary debt. These actions align with their deep-seated belief that they are only "meant" to earn $50,000.

Such subconscious behaviors are powerful because they continually steer the person back to their comfort zone of earning $50,000, which is what they truly believe they are worth. To break free from this cycle, they would need to change their beliefs about their own worthiness and potential, allowing them to strive for and achieve their higher financial goals.

The same self-sabotage principle holds true in any area of our life. For example, our beliefs about weight and fitness can act like an internal limit, affecting our habits and discipline.

Imagine someone who believes their natural, comfortable weight is 200 pounds. Even though they might dream of weighing 175 pounds and make plans to reach this goal, their deep-seated belief acts like a "health and fitness governor." They might stick to healthy habits for a while, having good days, weeks, or even months, as they try to get closer to their target weight.

However, their subconscious mind, which holds onto the belief that they are meant to weigh 200 pounds, can lead them back to old habits. They might start eating more junk food, skip workouts, or lose motivation without realizing why. These actions bring them back to their "comfortable" weight of 200 pounds, even when they consciously want to weigh less.

This cycle of setting a lower weight goal but being pulled back to 200 pounds demonstrates how self-sabotage can stem from our beliefs. Changing these beliefs is key to achieving lasting change. By shifting their mindset to truly believe they can be fit and healthy at 175 pounds, they can begin to break free from the habits that have kept them stuck, creating a new pattern of success and well-being.

Again, the governor can apply to any area of life. It can be the level of happiness you allow yourself to have in relationships or even at work. Some people believe that struggle and unhappiness is "normal." When things start going better than they believe they should be, they start to subconsciously self-sabotage to get back to the level they believe they are worthy of.

In order to overcome your self-sabotage, it is important to identify your current limiting beliefs. Complete the "Current Governors" exercise in the accompanying workbook before moving on to the next chapter. Becoming aware of the limiting thoughts you currently hold, will be extremely helpful information as you continue on your growth journey. Most people don't know themselves well enough or spend the time to find out how they are holding themselves back.

Remember that limits only exist in your mind. You can overcome self-sabotage and you have everything you need to do that NOW.

Great news! You are already eight chapters into creating new habits and making the right choices to shift your subconscious beliefs. The tools provided in this book, when consistently executed, will help you improve your self-belief and overcome any self-sabotage. Your self-worth can be found through faith and relationship with your Creator. Your self-confidence will grow as you stick to your new daily habits. Use your habit tracker daily and follow through with what you say you will do. Your self-esteem will continue to improve as you do your daily affirmations, manage your mindset, and achieve your goals.

It all starts with taking action and leveraging the tools provided every single day. Keep it simple and stay consistent. Focus on winning each day, then a year from now you will look up not even recognizing the person you are today. That is how much growth you will experience.

Action Items

Celebrate how far you have come! Keep your goals in front of you and stay committed (or recommit) to executing on your new daily habits.

Go to my website (formpowerfulhabits.com) to grab a free copy of my workbook to complete the "Current Governors" exercise from the "Believing in Yourself" chapter.

CHAPTER 9
Show Me Your Friends, I'll Show You Your Future

The Power of Your Circle

The saying "Show me your friends, and I'll show you your future" highlights the impact that those closest to us have on our lives. Studies suggest that we are the average of the five people we spend the most time with. This means that our closest friends influence our behavior, values, and even success in significant ways.

I had a friend once tell me about a lesson he shares with his kids about choosing friends wisely. He is an incredible father who creates a strong foundation of keeping God the center of their life and family. He tells his kids, "Your friends are either moving you closer to or farther away from God." When he shared that with me I thought, "Wow! That is so true and impactful!" Our friends are constantly pulling us in certain directions, whether we realize it or not.

Imagine you're part of a group of friends where everyone is health-conscious and regularly exercises. It's likely you will find yourself adopting healthier eating habits and joining in on physical activities, simply because you're influenced by their healthy behaviors. On the other hand, if your close friends tend to be more negative or discouraged, you might notice that their outlook begins to affect your mood and perspective, possibly leading you away from personal and professional success.

Consider a student who spends most of their time with friends who are dedicated to studying and achieving high grades. The student's environment is filled with motivation to learn, work hard, and achieve academic success. This supportive and ambitious circle makes it more likely for the student to mirror these behaviors, striving for similar achievements.

In contrast, if a person is surrounded by friends who often procrastinate or avoid their responsibilities, it becomes easier to adopt similar habits. This illustrates how the company we keep can direct our paths, either pushing us forward or holding us back from our potential. By choosing to spend time with people who exhibit positive and aspirational qualities, you align yourself on a path toward a brighter future.

Friends can either uplift or drag you down. They might inspire you to become a better spouse, parent, or leader, or conversely, they can steer you away from your goals, including your spiritual ones. Consider whether your friends energize you or if they sap your strength and joy. Are they the ones challenging you to reach higher, or are they poking holes in your boat, making it harder to keep afloat?

If you currently don't have enough people in your circle who are pulling you closer to where you want to be, you can start with reading books (like this one...look at you, winning!). Some other great mentors worth reading and following on social media are John Maxwell, Jack Canfield, Ed Mylett, Mel Robbins and Jon Gordon, to name a few. The more you can fill your mind with the things that give you energy to pursue a successful and impactful life, the more likely you are to reach your goals.

Like Attracts Like

We all wear many different hats. For example, I am a wife, mom, sister, daughter, niece, granddaughter, aunt, cousin, friend, leader, and mentor. Take a moment to reflect on all the different hats you wear. Now evaluate how you show up in those various relationships. Do you find yourself bringing positive energy, being an encourager and spreader of good news? Or might there be some relationships that center around complaining, negativity, and gossip? The reality is that there are some people who only know how to connect with others through negativity and gossip. However, that is not a healthy foundation for any relationship.

The concept of "like attracts like" is a gentle nudge to focus on self-improvement first. When you make an effort to become a better version of yourself, you naturally start to attract people who are also striving for growth and positivity. Just as a clean and organized space invites comfort, a person who works on self-betterment often draws in those who are on similar paths.

For example, if you are passionate about learning and personal development, as you begin to read more, attend workshops, or engage in meaningful conversations, you'll likely meet others who share these interests. These shared values and goals create a bond that encourages collective growth, making the journey enjoyable and fruitful.

On the flip side, it's important to recognize when certain relationships no longer serve your personal growth. If you surround yourself with people who have habits or mindsets that pull you back to an old version of yourself—perhaps one that wasn't healthy or constructive—it might be wise to spend less time with them. This doesn't have to mean ending friendships but rather prioritizing relationships that align with your current aspirations and values.

Remember, you cannot change anyone else, only yourself. A great place to start in attracting and fostering the right relationships is to show up as the best version of yourself. As you implement the tools in this book, that will naturally happen. You may need to give your closest friends and family members a heads-up that you are no longer going to be participating in the usual complaining and gossiping sessions. Let them know that you are being intentional about not poking holes in their boat. So where you may have normally called to tell them all the bad things that happened that day, you redirect the conversation to something positive, or don't make the phone call. It's like our mamas always say, "If you don't have anything nice to say, don't say anything at all."

If you've never read *The Energy Bus* by Jon Gordon, I highly recommend reading it. In the book, he talks about energy vampires and how to set a standard for not having them around. If you don't want to be around energy vampires, make sure you don't show up as one. The best way to do this is to eliminate gossip, complaining, and negativity. All three of those activities drain your energy and the energy of those around you.

There may be some energy vampires in your life who you can't avoid being around. Maybe it's a family member or a coworker at your job. I have been in a situation where someone close to me was almost unbearable for me to be around. Everything they did seemed to get under my skin and suck my energy. I decided to implement an exercise that worked wonders for me. I made the choice to intentionally catch that person doing something good or compliment them at least once every single day. I literally wrote this action item on my daily plan and checked it off once completed. In the beginning it was very challenging, and I sometimes had to reach to find something to compliment. As I stuck with it daily, it became easier to see the good.

As with anything, when you look for the good, the more good you will see. When I originally started this exercise, I thought it would change the other person's attitude and behavior. What I noticed was it actually ended up changing me and the way I viewed them. It transformed our relationship and the way I interacted with this person. I no longer harped on bad qualities or felt the need to vent about our encounters. It ultimately changed the energy I was bringing to the relationship, which in turn changed the energy I received from the relationship.

While this experience was transformative for me, it is important to note that it won't ultimately change the other person. But it will make it easier to be around them. You protect your own energy when you control what you are looking for and focusing on. By focusing on becoming the person you aspire to be, you'll naturally find yourself in the company of individuals who reflect and support your growth journey. This mutual encouragement builds a supportive network, helping everyone involved to reach their potential.

Iron Sharpens Iron

Growing up, my dad had this unforgettable saying: "An excuse is like a butthole, everybody's got one and they all stink!" I know, a bit gross, but incredibly effective. As a kid, this vivid imagery definitely made an impression and ensured I'd always think twice before making excuses. Please believe I am planting this same imagery in the minds of my children.

When we are falling short and making excuses, deep down we really don't want someone to call us out on it. We want people to validate our feelings and tell us it is okay. It is uncomfortable to be confronted. And, for most people, it is uncomfortable to be the one confronting your friend on their excuses. However, if we are going to grow, we must be willing to step outside of our comfort zones in order to help one another. Proverbs 27:17 says, "As iron sharpens iron, so one person sharpens another."

True friends are those who push you toward excellence. They don't always tell you what you want to hear; instead, they offer constructive criticism that helps you grow. Their goal is to build you up, not tear you down. Embrace these relationships, as they are essential for personal development. For example, a friend might point out areas where you're not performing your best, such as procrastinating on important tasks, not because they want to criticize you, but because they believe you can do better. Their constructive criticism comes from a place of love, care, and support, aiming to help you grow and improve. Accountability is something you do for someone, not to them.

Imagine you're working on a project (like completing the tools in this book), and a good friend (hopefully the accountability partner you chose at the beginning of the book) notices that you're stuck in a rut. Instead of simply agreeing and sympathizing, they might suggest new strategies or tools to help you progress, or even challenge you to set higher goals. Their intention is to push you toward excellence, building you up rather than tearing you down. Such relationships are catalysts for personal development, motivating you to take action and make improvements.

This principle of providing genuine feedback applies to every relationship but holds an even greater significance for those in leadership roles. If you have the privilege of leading others—whether at home, work, or within your community—it's your responsibility to recognize and nurture the potential in those around you. To achieve this, your observations and feedback must genuinely stem from a place of love and care. Effective leaders don't criticize harshly, nor do they simply tell people what they want to hear. In most cases it is easier not to have an accountability conversation or give feedback, but that does not serve those in your care. Be the leader that sees the best in them and is willing to invest in helping them live out their fullest potential.

Reflecting on my journey in corporate America, I noticed a trend: as I climbed higher up the ladder, more people tended to tell me only what they thought I wanted to hear. There was even a time when I found myself seeking validation for my opinions instead of pursuing honest feedback. This is a dangerous mindset, one that can hinder personal and professional growth. It's crucial for all of us to maintain self-awareness and remain open to receiving sincere feedback, as it enables us to show up as the best versions of ourselves.

As you continue your journey of creating your ideal future, it is crucial to evaluate the friendships in your life. Are the people around you encouraging your progress and celebrating your successes? Or are they content with seeing you remain in your comfort zone? By surrounding yourself with those who inspire and challenge you, you create an environment that supports your journey to becoming the best version of yourself. These friendships are not just beneficial—they are essential for reaching your potential and realizing your dreams.

CHAPTER 10
Conclusion —Make It Count

As you can now see from your journey in creating your ideal future, there are so many benefits of forming powerful habits. This path is not about a finite destination. It is a journey filled with new opportunities and chapters waiting to be explored. Creating your ideal future starts by cultivating the life you wish to lead right now, through intentional choices and actions that align with your values and goals. You're creating a lifestyle and experiencing life differently through the choices you make. It is about who you become in the process of pursuing excellence. The last chapter of this book is not an ending but rather a new beginning in your personal narrative. Think of it as an exciting transition into a new future brimming with potential and purpose.

My hope is that you feel more equipped than ever before to make lasting changes in your life now that you have accomplished the following:

- ✓ Solidified an accountability partner: Let them know how they can continue to partner with you on this journey
- ✓ Clarified your ideal future
- ✓ Identified your current/old habits that are not serving you
- ✓ Completed your Goals Worksheet for two or three SMART goals that move you closer to your ideal future
- ✓ Identified which daily habits will help you achieve your goals and create your ideal future
- ✓ Tracking your new daily habits
- ✓ Learned how to change your mental channel when overcoming negativity
- ✓ Created positive self-talk through speaking daily affirmations one or two times per day
- ✓ Learned how to leverage self-belief to overcome self-sabotage

You have the tools you need. Now it is up to you to take consistent action! Odds are you've made it all the way to the end of this book because you are implementing the tools and progressing on your journey. Kudos to you! If you find you are still struggling with some of the above items, it is still worth celebrating that you have come this far. Keep going and don't give up!

None of us were called to live a life of mediocrity. *You* were meant for more. Believe that, own it, and walk in it! We are all creators. We all have the power to create a life we are proud to lead! We now know how our choices and habits play a vital role in that. You know what kind of life you want to live and have solidified that vision with clarity. That already puts you far ahead of the majority of people aimlessly roaming through life.

Make It Count

First, it's crucial to focus on ourselves by making our own choices, developing good habits, and being disciplined. This self-leadership is a vital starting point. However, many other people also need these same skills to better their lives. As we discussed, it's important to understand that we can't change others; they must desire change themselves and be ready to take necessary actions. With that being said, I truly believe there are many who want a better life. They know there's a better way and that they need to make better choices, but some may not know how. Often, they find themselves caught in a cycle of inconsistency, which can lead to feelings of guilt and a negative self-image. This can result in a pattern of self-sabotage, leaving them asking why they haven't progressed further in life. But it doesn't have to be this way. I believe that anyone who commits to using these tools can make significant positive changes in their future.

However, a major issue is that not enough people are sharing these messages of hope in the world. Many are engulfed in negativity, choosing instead to engage in heated discussions about politics or the economy. They might complain about issues without taking responsibility or trying to change them. Remember what I said about "Show me your friends and I'll show you your future?" If we surround ourselves with certain types of people, won't we naturally become like them? Or worse, if we are those people, aren't we just creating more of them? Kinda scary, right? As humans, we're connected in many ways, especially through the energy we project.

That's why it's important to adhere to successful, intentional habits. These habits protect our energy and influence how we show up in the world. Now is the time to invite others on this path by spreading messages of hope. Indeed, anyone can create the life they desire by following straightforward processes. But if people don't know about these simple steps, they will continue living in a world filled with negativity and distractions. Let's help change that together by being part of the solution and spreading hope!

Identify two or three people that you believe could benefit from this book and share it with them. Then work together on your goal worksheets, habit trackers, and creating your morning routine. Also, commit to one another that you will hold each other accountable to changing the channel when you need to overcome negative thinking. If you and your accountability partner stick to this challenge daily for ninety days, send me an email at info@formpowerfulhabits.com letting me know how this impacted you. If you don't see drastic differences in your energy and the way you show up in life at the end of the ninety days, I will refund your money for this book. I have been living these values and implementing these tools for years, and I am extremely confident that they will work for you, but only if you work the process *consistently*. The best way to learn something is to teach it. Pulling in an accountability partner or group will only help you stick to the process and master it.

Living as the best version of yourself and embracing your God-given purpose is like becoming a beacon of light for others. When you follow your path of choosing habits that create your ideal future, you inspire those around you by showing them what is possible. By living your purpose, you serve as a role model, showing how fulfilling life can be when you align with your true self. Imagine your life as a trail you are blazing through a forest, making it easier for others to find their way.

Furthermore, by inviting others on this journey you are helping them find their own path. Your invite just might be the bridge built for them to cross into new opportunities, empowering them to reach their full potential. Together, these actions create a ripple effect of goodness, spreading positivity and encouraging everyone to live a life filled with intention and purpose. This way, your legacy becomes a significant influence, encouraging a community of empowered individuals. It starts with you.

www.ingramcontent.com/pod-product-compliance
Lightning Source LLC
Chambersburg PA
CBHW050657160426
43194CB00010B/1972